urban disorders

poems by

Natasha N. Deonarain

Finishing Line Press
Georgetown, Kentucky

urban disorders

To Roger.
You. And I.
We know.

Copyright © 2022 by Natasha N. Deonarain
ISBN 978-1-64662-873-5 First Edition
All rights reserved under International and Pan-American Copyright Conventions.
No part of this book may be reproduced in any manner whatsoever without written permission from the publisher, except in the case of brief quotations embodied in critical articles and reviews.

ACKNOWLEDGMENTS

Harbinger Asylum: "urban disorders"
Juked: "rampage"
What Rough Beast: "Quarantine"
The Writing Disorder: "The plot continues without them"
Prometheus Dreaming: "Moroccan Baby Shaker"
GNU Journal: "Truth is a dragonfly"
Canyon Voices Spring 2019: "Pink Ladies" and "115°F"
Door = Jar: "Le Baiser"
Connecticut River Review: "Days like"
Permafrost: "Afternoon Meditation"
Swamp Ape Review: "jasper national park"
Crack the Spine Literary Magazine: "Corpus Diem"
The RavensPerch: "Yoga for Dummies"
Dissident Voice: "Leftovers and Takeaways"
Poetry for Living Waters: "Gaia"

"social distancing" was published in *Poems from the Lockdown* (Willowdown Books, 2020).

"there's a crash on I-25 this route avoids all traffic delays click yes to continue" was published in *Fun House*, Volume 43, Issue 1 by Pilgrimage Press.

"Indigo Sky" was published in the *Little Red Tree International Poetry Prize 2012 Anthology*.

"Gaia" won second prize in the 5th Annual Chandler-Gilbert Community College Stand and Deliver Poetry Slam Competition 2013.

Publisher: Leah Huete de Maines
Editor: Christen Kincaid
Cover Art and Design: Rebecca Thompson Design
Author Photo: Pablo Robles, Media Compass Photography

Order online: www.finishinglinepress.com
also available on amazon.com

Author inquiries and mail orders:
Finishing Line Press
PO Box 1626
Georgetown, Kentucky 40324
USA

Table of Contents

urban disorders 1

rampage 2

city 'scape 4

Quarantine 8

social distancing 9

The plot continues without them 10

Moroccan Baby Shaker 13

how to save the children : 14

Truth is a dragonfly 15

pink ladies 16

Le Baiser 17

Boat at sea, 1894 18

Days like 19

115°F 20

Afternoon Meditation 21

jasper national park 22

front range 23

there's a crash on I-25 this route avoids all traffic delays click yes to continue 24

too late 25

Corpus Diem 27

Yoga for Dummies 29

Leftovers and Takeaways 30

Gaia 31

Indigo Sky 33

urban disorders

binge netflix—
fist-stuff slapstick down your throat, the tell;
a million boinks on the head with happy endings until it comes up
over red-raw knuckles—
brush acid from your teeth with sense-o-dyne,
put on a chipmunk's smile when you
dream of fatted calf, roasted lamb—
mint juleps sipped on a patio home by the sea,
gazing at mercurial waters, chewing half-baked fish,
the finger-fed taste of unleavened bread—
roll stone from your refrigerator door at breakfast,
shivering left-overs, a weeping steak—
anything to feed the blood-thirsty hound.

rampage

I'm happy now I believe that I'm happy now and yes I'm happy now
    I've got all that I want that I need that I want
        I've got
        everything that I want when I need when I want a
            peck on the lips hello a goodbye brush so light a
            touch that might lie after 20 years logical calculated
            separation of love's measures
        as the years go by—

clutched on the bed on the floor on the couch
    by the skin by the sweat and the pant it's too much
    it's too deep inside
        look at me deep inside
            put it deep inside and there inside
                it won't split like yolk from the white
                or the sound—

            it's the sound
            it's every sound that he makes
        it's a high-pitched hum
on my drums on the drum
it's the drum that I mind in my mind every rise
        every step every drop
that escapes when it scrapes my skin it's a three-pronged rake
drawing blood mixing blood with the dishes stacked high

on Saturday night spitting blood piling high
and the bills piling high paper throats getting slit
spitting blood
spitting dues and their dates and these ticks off our lives
    while this garbage piles high
        and the bills and the plates where I swallow my diatribe
            like a fistful of Vicodin
            chased by a shot
            where we each take a shot it's a shot—

but the doctor's too rude
won't make me happy no more
I'll be happy with more when I hear the garage down
    at 9 am up
    and 6 pm down
    and it's up and it's down and it's nine and it's six
    and it's nine and six-nine-six-nineninenineninewellbefine

and every time
    every goddamn time a peck on the lips when
    I'm barely touched
        when the distance in sheets or in beds or in rooms
        spreads to a hotel door
        screaming he's a good man he's a real honest man
he's my hard working man and I'm happy now I believe that
I'm happy now

and there's nothing more that I fucking want

city 'scape

i.

steampunk world   dark
    winter
      wonderland   exposed
copper wires of our anxieties   motherboard
memories from an opioid haze

there's garbage all over this place

mask
glove
lysol®

no one to replace our empty shelves shorn
of this hefty responsibility

stand alone

      at the corner of van buren and jefferson   gaze at
tumbleweeds gathering on cracked tar   living inside
crumbling
concrete walls that smell of iron and wine

      utopia's not a place we dream about
        it's the fate of our time

ii.

she screams

        at the hopeless from the top of her stack stuffing feed
    into upturned palms and a little bit of something else
for tomorrow's today

    it hasn't rained here in 40 days and 40 nights—
quite right you should stay
        when everyone else has gone astray—

iii.

utopia's not some safe space
on a leafy campus

    it's a right to li(f)e

iv.

let's turn off the tv shall we   time to wake up   dream
        all that can be

        take no comfort in endless exhaust pipe babble
    that froth into the furry air amidst a
landscape of piercings and blue ink where lack
        has become our brand

regress the rest
don't travel time
it's not possible to get all this done
without a capsule   listen—

I say ditch the carnivore
and his meatless cravings   rive entitlements
from the bone   gnash it
with your dulling   fangs

no my friend   you're not alone

v.

hiding behind you the taste of common   sense lingers
on my lips   salts my tongue but stupidity

          won't let itself be quarantined when
          everyone's still a headcase packed with pills and your
brother who married a walking vagina insists—

suicide is trending now on twitter so you'd better act or
your dog will become the worst of you—

          we've never been this close before

vi.

freedom was a guy I once knew but he died
in a fatal car crash last year and now studies say that
twerking is more dangerous than mass
times the velocity of light squared so look—

we need a new mantra

a basket case filled with hulu's and stale beer
          why suffer a head of schedule

        silence
        was sold out a long time ago so as we journey
on
        we'll make our living picking things—
plastic things with plastic smiles washed up on plastic shores
    and I must say these days

   driftwood takes on a new meaning

when meaning is a dark voided out and   thoughts
have become fossilized under thick layers of desert
    dust   now rust rings
        your day your month your year doesn't it

well   nevermind—
let's just exchange vows right now   promise
each other that once upon a time—
        we'll become the news

Quarantine

I stifle a cough—
hand flies to my mouth like a hasty surgical mask but
it's too late;
your accusing eyes turn on me and widen, sink to the depths
of your cloth-bound frown. Heat

rushes to my cheeks mistaken for three degrees above normal
and it's time to quarantine—

they say.

Too bad my allergies are terrible this year;
eyes wet, inflamed, nose dew in a slow drip
to the top of my lip like tankers in the street but I'll not
wipe it away. I'll suck it all
up and gulp down
my mucusy pride. I'll stare off into the distance
toward some invisible enemy casually adrift, lounging
on a droplet in air—

I'll finger
my cuts and scrapes from last night's toilet roll rumble
that made this pain
worthwhile.

But from behind a frenzied laptop my friend,
I long for your touch, the
feel of your smile,
the nestling heat of your body and sound of your undigitized voice—

a tap of a stainless steel knife against a crystal glass
calling us to attention, a remembered
past when we were way too drowsy to see
what might have been.

social distancing

speak to me—
tell me the textured story I long to hear, to see
what isn't there but don't
open your mouth; your words are potent drops of venom
dangling in this biting air & we've been told
by powers that be to stay

six feet away—

we can't touch anymore—
but should I be shunned to say I ache for the tight clasp of your
fingers
in mine, unspoken words that held & would never
let go (but did) & would I be wrong
to whisper that I want so much the bouldered foundation of your
smile;

a bordered wall around just you & me?

now I can only imagine what's behind your mask,
what's hidden inside
this electric screen of distorted images I receive, yet I can still
remember
the breath of our laughter once—
mixed together as multiformed icicles in skating rink air
when we
turned & twirled, arms outstretched & the world
only a blur but tell me—

when this is all over, will we find each other again?

The plot continues without them

[Scene 1]
Must I endure your hiccups? It's not enough
to want darkly,
you should want me, adorable nightmare.
When the crows
discovered the murder, he left home with a broken
wing but unlike us, lions will never give up
their pride

[Scene 2]
or goats their kids. Every
new day is a fresh homicide, fear and loathing
aren't required
for the plot to continue. Snakes
build nests but don't fly so you really shouldn't
get drunk at the feast.
Someone is bound to betray you
after I speak my confession
to the praying mantis, but forgiveness hasn't been
invented yet; we still live amongst the
unkindness of ravens.
Dandelions send helicopter drones to spy

[Scene 3]
on the swollen desert
(without healthcare benefits, of course)
but my hard-boiled legacy, cut from rapture
when the Yangtze River
was still an irreversible wonder, has no place
when the backdrop changes
color.
Look, if you have a question, don't
be afraid
to hold up your hand—
receive and you shall ask.

Its will is done
if you so name it, for when you allow
the Book to open, it falls to the correct page.
She doesn't like
your charms, but
to a fox, water's your best friend

[Scene 4]

or your worst enemy. It all depends on hindsight.
Is the stairway to Heaven paved in stone, you ask?
It depends
on how far this pavement goes
but be careful, no matter
how far they let go, sonar always brings them
home. Should I call You Mister or Missus, then?
The Gardener doesn't know if crimson
will be in style this year,
but pay what you owe. He'll
decide the price later since this
journey's not done. The lightness of being is insatiable
yet we still hide truth

[Scene 5]

under our pillows
in the quiet's night air. Remember—
don't take the shortcut or
you'll be cut short this time, like lonely cows in a lonely field
that really don't feel lonely when they stand and face the
pelting storm, so you should easily find

[End]

your own compass through this dark matter and other such physics particles. Shards of glass embedded in your skin don't hurt but you still feel their hurt. It's the business of ferrets that you're too concerned with so rather adopt an attitude of shrewdness like a few apes with whom you're well acquainted. Oh for Heaven's sake, why should all this be such a mystery to you?

Moroccan Baby Shaker

The girl he married rattles her baby at night because he won't settle for a nap. In snapshots, she covers seaweed eyes with honey-dripping hair, hunched faceless, shrouding a button-faced toddler with a potent veil. He peaks from below, startled, unaware but determined, she thrusts her fist toward probing lights, fingers heavy with jagged rock. Thumb and hooked baby tug away from each other in a hang-ten sign that rips apart the palm of her heart who doesn't yet know what to do about the girl he married.

how to save the children :

; started in a three bedroom house
with a great yard for the kids, awesome
master bath and finished basement when we
                                      [   ]
; had to switch to this third floor apartment
but it was okay really, the kids could share
a bedroom and those
                                      [   ]
; neighbors drove us crazy so we thought
why not just get a van, how easy
would it be to never sit in traffic or
maybe, we could park right outside
                                      [   ]
; when we heard about this hot
architect making a killing by building
these houses in alleys and keeping
the price
                                      [   ]
; as low as possible when all you
really need is three or four
hundred square feet, a metal train car
storage unit and we'd be saving so much
                                      [   ]
; if we just move down the street where
they've put up tents but before you say anything
give me a chance, they're just hard-working
                                      [   ]
; people who'd set up an office right there
between those cars in that parking
space downtown and you'd be so close
to home you'd see the kids every
                                      [ ]
; day when I'm in the grocery store
and she keeps asking if I'd like to donate
my bag fee to save the children so I said
                                      [ ]

Truth is a dragonfly

Truth is a dragonfly dying on your patio first thing in the morning
and you don't know what to do
so you take a picture of its stage makeup face—
velvet eyes and iridescent purple tail,
sun glinting through cracked glass wings.

You think about sending the picture
to your sister
whom you haven't spoken to for years ever since that time—
but then you think it's just too exhausting
to click the share icon on your cell
and press send just as it was so exhausting

to ask her to join you for a cup of coffee or grab some lunch
all those years ago and her
demanding payment before she'd agree
and besides—

it's probably raining
wherever she is right now so you watch
until his leg stops twitching and he lies there perfectly still

and then you walk into the kitchen to make a cup of tea.

pink ladies

some hang there, crawling back into and through
themselves, shrinking their bodies to be as faint as possible
so they'll never have to fall.

others let go, free-fall until they land
hard with a thud. they won't let their bruises heal but prefer
instead to rot, making it as unpleasant as possible
for everyone else to endure.

some like a bit of s&m. they get a bite bit from
their taut flesh, bemoaning pain and pleasure,
watching plump lips and canines drip sweet juice.

those who wait are caught by caressing hands and
carried away in baskets of glory, carefully placed
on top of tables and inside crystalline bowls where
their life is painted into stillness.

Le Baiser
after Pablo Picasso, 1969

You bring me
this bowl of voluptuous cherries—
dimpled, dark-skinned, taut;
attempt to feed away my fears.

You say,
take these words; dangle them
over the tip of your tongue,
taste their bittersweet nectar that swells
both sides of your cheeks,
squeezes briny streams into the basin
of your plump pout.

You hold my confession in your gnarled mouth,
chiseled canines awash in crimson juice and
wait until I swallow my silence
like a drying pit—

fragments of flesh tongued from Rubenesque bones.

Boat at sea, 1894

"The movement of natural elements cannot be captured by the brush: to paint lightning, a gust of wind, or the splash of a wave from nature is inconceivable."
—Ivan Aivazovsky

It's dark
Here raindrops shatter
Against this phone box glass
Rattle the metal bones of my cage
Claw their way inside your
Silence at
The end of the line
We've been painted
A sort of yellowing gray
Inside this gilded frame
I'm a scrawl on the
Lower right corner
Of your Pythagorean mind I'm
Drowning
In the foaming lips of a
Tongueless sea but
I wonder was
Our blood simply
A Mistake on Canvas
Oil painted rejections
Of congealed illusions
Meant to keep us
Forever
Inside this gilded frame?

Days like

This.　I want to describe.　In real words.　But even that.　Would change.　How I feel.　Now.　If you pressed.　Me I'd say.　It's like watching.　A nude.　Standing.　Toes curled around the. Stone edge.　Of a sheer cliff.　It's like she leans.　Forward.　And seagulls swoop.　Behind her.　In and out.　Of invisible cracks. Tucked between.　Those tall cliff.　Walls.　And you feel nothing. It's like something falls.　A small, dark spectacle.　Falling in front. Of the sky.　It's like she falls.　To the ground.　And she makes. No sound.

115°F

I forgot how you made me feel that day, trying
to remember but it was so long ago. A thousand
cactus needles stuck deep in every pore until
I stood with my arms waving motionless in the acrid
air, rotting from the inside out. In the desert, we make
furniture from skeletons we find in the dust, carefully
plucking flesh from bone. But there's no ceremony before
or after. We simply use and reuse, each aspect a colorful
reincarnation of one source. Now, I remember how
you made me feel.

Afternoon Meditation

On the convex edge of horizons, many miles
across this bone-flat desert, dust pulls
a Navajo blanket around her
swollen belly.

200,000 years gestation and still no birth;
only our uncommon let down.

When will a new age begin? We've
waited with empty stomachs for a second coming
to tear down these walls,

let a little sun
shine onto our drying husks, entangled cobwebs
brushed from every bordered zone.

Maybe we should recycle our own hot air,
or wipe out these carbon footprints so no one can follow,
seal the deal fair and green.

One day, this tsunami will eat us all.
Some day, we'll become two-toned geckos cutting through dirt,
heads black,
tails white,
scaling promises we cannot see.

Billions of bickering voices echo from
electronically-boxed canyons and in the distance, the
muted sounds of a rattler
warning us—

It's time to move on.

jasper national park
dedicated to s.d.

edge of a cliff. viewpoint ahead;
stiff upper lip of an abyss
moustached with unshaven pine,
opens one groggy red eye.

motor kills. young family
spills from four doors of a white mercedes;
three children unleashed, flapping, clapping,
this way that when—

a shudder. father spots her
unsteady on diaper-bound legs rocking, rocking;
cavernous mouth yawning below.

dry lips pinch. no air dare escape and he,
keenly aware if he grabs,
makes one sudden move,
she'll clap flap up down so instead reaches
fingers, thumb to breast pocket, shakes a ring of shiny keys;
    come, look what I have here for you!

attention caught. she bares four white teeth,
takes one rickety step back as wife, crystallized,
sinks polished nails
deep into youngest boy's flesh.

now. narcissists in full bloom,
roots deep, soiled and tended by time;
if one more step—
what difference in our lives would she have
chosen
to make?

front range

mountains yawn
swallow me whole

inside bowels
I'm broken

protons
become waves

waves stitch
fascia to rock
trabeculae

soon I am
a mountain

soon I am

not me

there's a crash on I-25 this route avoids all traffic delays click yes to continue

we moved to high ground after
setting fire to the valley, watched it torch everything
in its wake—

white tail retreated, hiding behind piñons;
our Coloradan housing projects burning every bulrush, feather
reed clump and Golden Boulder,

spreading quickly to the base where its frenzy

licked at the unsewn hems of dark skirts,
igniting lodgepoles until aspens, cloaked in green sequins,
quaked beside weeping juniper—

its smoke overstaying a lukewarm welcome
in blizzards and bomb cyclones,
hanging so low our tweets couldn't put it out,

regret rising thick, suffocating;
every agonal breath a sentinel
sedated so deeply we couldn't hear anymore

so we just stood there not knowing what to do in the freeze
until we couldn't see
our own hands in front of our noses.

too late

*

colorado foothills
under infectious consumption you stand at the door
our intersection of blood and wire
    you turn to me
    look through me

skin me alive
    I want to change your mind but I know
not this time not ever again

*

my ache
my congenital grief
the browning edges of my desire
the burnt landscape of my desperation
    still
you say nothing

*

I'm a pelt
choked around your neck
stroked endlessly stoked with love
one that you loved

how should I feel love
inside this narcissistic epidemic

*

where's my symbol
my gold won from all that I hate
all that's gone wrong

      between you and me what we should
have been to each other
anyway   now
or is it too late

*

haunted
      silent   still
I'm hunted
      not by you
      not by who

      I'd beg for you to stay but how
do I start at the end

end

*

you stood near the tree
under unforgiving lights
at the visitor's center
      pale   drawn

I searched your eyes
one last time as the owl
      dived
talons   wide
as the owl   glared
I found your stare but you were
already gone
                      gone

Corpus Diem

There's no shame in carrying around a Dead Body;
anyone with any claim to equal rites
seems to have one these days.

Used to be you'd leave your dearly departed
in the back of your closet amongst relics and skeletons,
being considerate not to lament
his last words in public,
but now that they're all out, large deposits of remains
get spread out over every conceivable safe space.

This Cadaveric Craze has swept the nation,
finding many people who are willing to take
good care of their undead; willing to
feed and clothe them every day,
let them out for a breath of fresh air once in a while,
bring them to mummy's office or to school for tell and show.

Some even escort them around airports,
pointing proudly to their
Bright Red Vests, or dress them up and
take them on dinner dates
to barebones restaurants buried inside downtown
and suburban streets—

just about anywhere large congregations
are found.

At any given time and in any given place,
more inanimates are present than fully alive,
pickled so strikingly well
it becomes virtually impossible to tell the difference
between the living and the half-baked.

There still exists, however, a few unfortunates
who see dead people everywhere,
but as a general rule, these irreverants are quickly
pronounced afflicted with a terminal illness,
heavily medicated and conveniently
kick the can,
providing opportunity for us to be reminded
that yet another untouchable problem
has been put to rest
with a quick fix.

If you one day decide you're sick and tired
of your stiff and would like to let him go,
all you have to do is pry his cold, dead hands
from around your neck,
tell him his services are no longer needed
and forthwith,
your beloved will turn to ash, leaving you quite free
to get on with your life.

Yoga for Dummies

In this pose, stretch until you fall apart.
In this pose, fall into a dark matter.
In this pose, learn that nothing is as it seems.
In this pose, make a plea bargain.
In this pose, option to become a delusion or a distraction.
Hold for 10 breaths.
In this pose, forgive all his intrusions.
In this pose, let go of your stamp collection.
In this pose, render yourself useless.
In this pose, fine tune your vocal chords.
In this pose, stuff all worldly gifts into a red stiletto.
In this pose, grow a thick skin.
In this pose, become a psychosomatic corpse.
In this pose, send all regrets to front.
In this pose, send all regrets to back.
In this pose, click control alt delete.
In this pose, never let them see you sweat.

Leftovers and Takeaways

Take away the agenda
Take away the exchange
Take away our climate
Take away its change

Take away abortion
Take away the rights
Take away the terrorist
Take away the fights

Take away university
Take away their thugs
Take away this perversity
Take away its drugs

Take away the racist
Take away the race
Take away the color
Take away our hate

Take away pretending
Take away our cake
Take away our ending and please—
Take away our fate

Gaia

Mother. Humble, we kneel at your feet touching once, twice, thrice and ask that you accept these token offerings our insatiable appetites emerge sightless, senseless into form birthed from the fertile soils of your womb to feed gaping gullets with unconditional love as only a mother could.

Caress our face, your fingertips to lips we ask of you much more and so shall you give.

Madre. When piety sinks to ocean depths in rock and so cannot be contained we drill for blackened soup as sustenance our goblets flow with heart blood rise to blanket watery sins with multi-hued suffocate slick in brilliant sun our briny alter to your steadfast love.

Kiss soft our cheeks and shed no tear for we are your chosen and so shall we take.

Maman. Homage to silver pulp stored in silicon lock and key seep arsenical through glistening skin we strip your body bare and give you back such forms of carbon lust our just exchange for effluent love the air we breathe unable to stop this mad pursuit we fall on grounded knee and cry aloud for you.

Hold close ourselves unto your breast can you now see how thus we are so lost?

Maji. We anoint the center of your heart our plastic jewel so placed to swirl through currents of time and space compounded waste of countless lives to gather thus and uncontained as foul in drifting seas it swells our gifts of love for we are yours through flesh and blood these bonds cannot be cut.

Your whisper still resounds inside this fading light we cup so dear inside our palm.

Ma.   Filled with rot from wired lives we're blind and so see naught but nuclear dust on golden eyes our gratitude glows against cobalt skies the platinum curls of angelic hair please take this garland of our shard and drape your throat so thus constrict your beauty reigns.

       You reach but cannot touch our sense and so we turn in shade our sacred contracts broke.

Mana.   We your incubus by natural law must love and thus with each day passed we press our dying hands in paralyzed awe and bow in reverent prayer you asked for naught but our respect through all this time and this we could not give.

       Is it too late this sinking sun that sets our souls to dark?

Ama.   Through dried brush plain and ochre red your kaleidoscope we tear your clothes and leave you charred in burning fire may we remember all that is and no longer here for us to love our folly consumes but ma! You taught us naught and doomed to endless rhyme the past forgot.

       This cycle must we repeat unchecked unchained for those to come?

Destroy.
Matris.
Forgive us please we beg of you for we knew not.
And we could not attempt to Be—

Another way.

Indigo Sky

> *"Mon cher, je t'adore. Sans commencement et sans fin, je t'adore."*

Caught between flesh and bone my body presses to yours—
Heart on heart.
I smell the perfume of your sweet skin. Still.
The spot where the tip of my nose
Brushes your neck you—
Turn to me.

I long to tell you the songs from my life transcended through time and space
Catapulted to this clumsy existence between
Shadows of him and her.

But what does it all mean?

I'm tortured by your presence. Still.
Electric, consuming, igniting joy and anguish
You—

And I.
We should know.

Trapped in hide and hair we don't—
Know.

Without this meaningless whisper silent lips part over soundless word we don't—
Know.

Is it The Knowing at a midnight hour when we hear what we want
And nothing more?

Outside this room waves lick the tender lips of sand and smile,
A lover's candied kiss under an indigo sky and stars—
Of infinite possibility.

There was love before you came.
There will be love after you go.

But in this formidable moment
This insignificant breath of existence
Those words simply must be said or rapture dissolves without them.

Ecstasy cannot stay.

Under the weight of your body I drop to non-existence
I fracture to infinity and suddenly there is no beginning and no end—

You. And I.
We know.

Natasha N. Deonarain is a graduate of the University of Alberta Faculty of Medicine. In addition to being a physician, poet and entrepreneur, she's the author of *The 7 Principles of Health* (Persephone's Publishing, 2013), a call for Americans to live better lives in health consciousness, and her first poetry chapbook, *50 études for piano* (Assure Press Publishing, 2021). She's also the recipient of the 2020 Three Sisters Award by *NELLE* magazine and was a recent nominee for Best of the Net by *Rogue Agent Journal* (2020).

Natasha has owned and operated multiple successful brick and mortar and online businesses and is the co-founder of a non-profit organization that seeks to rebuild the trusting relationship between police and their communities (*www.prefundthepolice.org*).

An avid swimmer, skier, figure skater and accomplished pianist, she's traveled extensively around the world and enjoys creative cooking. Find her recipes in her forthcoming book, *dystopian cuisine* (Persephone's Publishing, 2021).

In her spare time, Natasha can be found staring off into space, contemplating her relationship between science and spirit.

www.ingramcontent.com/pod-product-compliance
Lightning Source LLC
LaVergne TN
LVHW041505070426
835507LV00012B/1347